TINY STITCHES

The Life of Medical Pioneer Vivien Thomas

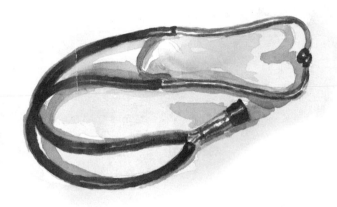

by Gwendolyn Hooks

Illustrated by Colin Bootman

Lee & Low Books Inc. • New York

Needles didn't scare Vivien Thomas. In fact, he designed the ones lying on the operating table in front of him. The instruments were small and delicate, like a toy. But these needles weren't toys. In a few hours, they would help save the life of a little girl.

Vivien checked the instruments carefully. They were sterilized, razor sharp, and ready for a brand-new type of operation that Vivien had invented. If it worked, the little girl would live to crawl, play, and grow strong like other children.

But would the operation work?

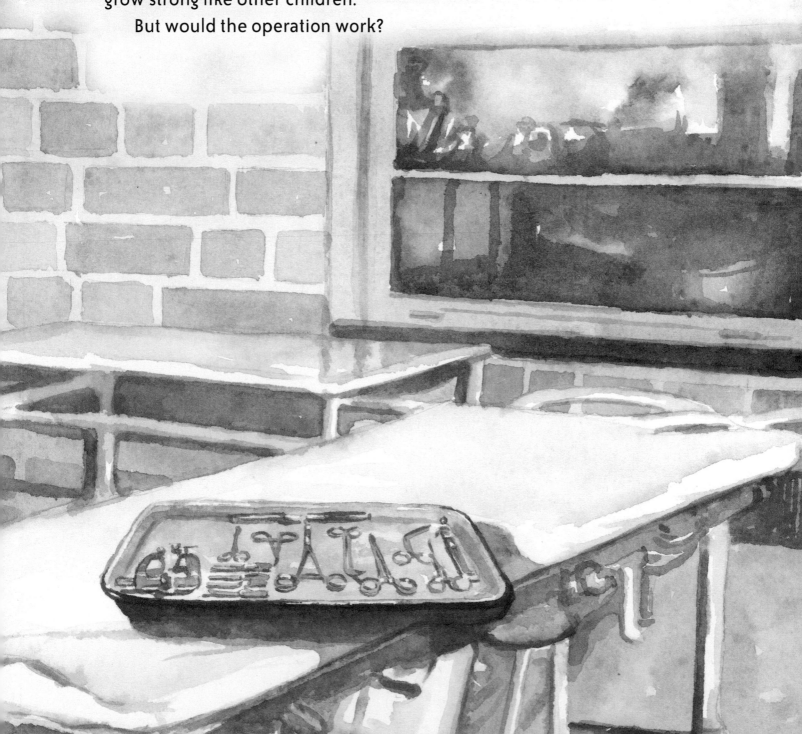

Vivien Theodore Thomas grew up in Nashville, Tennessee. Vivien's father was a master carpenter who taught his son how to measure, cut, and seamlessly fit together pieces of wood. By the age of thirteen, Vivien was working alongside his father and earning enough money to buy his own clothes and shoes. He put the rest of his money in a bank to save for college.

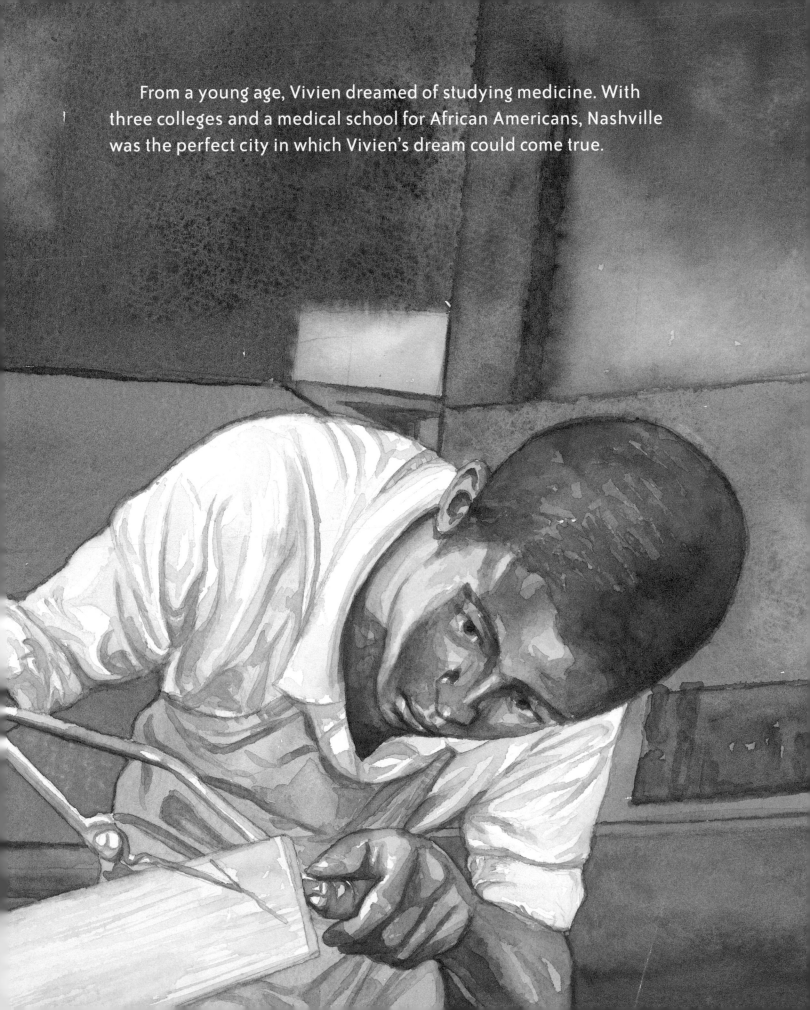

From a young age, Vivien dreamed of studying medicine. With three colleges and a medical school for African Americans, Nashville was the perfect city in which Vivien's dream could come true.

In October 1929, the stock market crashed and the Great Depression that followed caused panic, hardship, and heartache throughout the United States. Banks lost their customers' savings and were forced to close. Vivien was one of the unlucky people who lost all his money. He had to start saving for college all over again.

Jobs were scarce for carpenters such as Vivien and his father. People could no longer afford to buy new houses or repair old ones. Luckily, one of Vivien's friends worked at Vanderbilt University and knew about a job opening at the medical school. Vanderbilt was an all-white university. Vivien knew that the school would never admit him as a student, but he hoped working there meant he was getting closer to his dream of studying medicine.

The next day, Vivien met with Dr. Alfred Blalock about the job. After a brief interview, Dr. Blalock took Vivien on a tour of the lab.

Chemical smells tickled Vivien's nose. His fingers itched to touch the equipment with fascinating names such as spirometer and blood-gas manometer. Dr. Blalock said he needed someone he could "teach to do anything I can do and maybe do things I can't do."

Vivien listened carefully as Dr. Blalock talked about his research projects. One of the projects captured Vivien's attention. Dr. Blalock explained that if a person was seriously injured and lost a lot of blood, his or her body sometimes went into shock. This meant the person's blood pressure became dangerously low because too little blood flowed to the body's organs, such as the heart and lungs. This often led to the patient dying. Dr. Blalock was researching treatments for these shock patients.

As Vivien listened, he also asked questions about the different procedures the doctor had tried. Dr. Blalock was impressed with Vivien and offered him the job right away.

On Vivien's first day at work, Dr. Blalock asked him to put an animal to sleep to prepare for a shock experiment. Vivien was uncomfortable with the idea of using animals for research, but Dr. Blalock explained that their research could save thousands of lives. So Vivien weighed the animal and calculated how much medicine it needed to fall into a deep, painless sleep. Then he set up the blood pressure equipment.

Under Dr. Blalock's supervision, Vivien learned to conduct experiments and write lab reports detailing each step. Dr. Beard, another doctor in the lab, loaned Vivien medical textbooks. He told Vivien, "It was nice to be able to do a thing, but it was better to know why you are doing it."

It wasn't long before Vivien was completing experiments from start to finish on his own.

Vivien's surgical techniques improved with each operation. Just as he had learned to fit pieces of wood together seamlessly, Vivien learned to suture, or sew, blood vessels together seamlessly. Dr. Blalock was impressed by Vivien's tiny stitches. Sometimes Vivien assisted Dr. Blalock with an experiment. On other days, Dr. Blalock assisted Vivien.

Vivien was happy working as a researcher, until he learned that his official job description was janitor. White men with the same duties and skills as Vivien were called research technicians and earned more money. Vivien was insulted. He was not a janitor. He told Dr. Blalock that he would not continue working unless he was paid the same as the other technicians. A few days later, Vivien noticed his paycheck was much better. He now earned about the same as the white technicians.

In 1941, Johns Hopkins Hospital in Baltimore, Maryland, invited Dr. Blalock to become Chief of Surgery. He accepted with one condition—his research technician, Vivien Thomas, must be invited too. Vivien didn't want to leave Nashville, but he knew he would be fired from Vanderbilt as soon as Dr. Blalock left. Many of the other doctors were not happy that Vivien had been working independently as a researcher.

Vivien accepted Dr. Blalock's offer. He was excited to start his new job at Johns Hopkins as Surgical Technician in Research. But Vivien had a hard time finding a nice home for his family in Baltimore. The better houses and apartments were for "whites only." It took months for Vivien to find an apartment.

Johns Hopkins was much more segregated than Vanderbilt. There were "whites only" and "colored" cafeterias and restrooms in the hospital. Vivien was the only African American working as a researcher. The stares and whispers in the hallways were worse than at Vanderbilt. But Vivien refused to let the prejudice of others interfere with his work.

In 1943, Dr. Helen Taussig, a pediatric cardiologist, visited Dr. Blalock's lab. Dr. Taussig treated children with heart problems. Many of her patients were born with a heart defect that made their skin look bluish. Their bodies did not get enough oxygen, and over time the children died. Dr. Taussig called these small patients her "blue babies."

Most doctors refused to do open-heart surgery on a child. They believed children couldn't survive such an operation. Even so, Dr. Taussig asked Dr. Blalock to find a way to operate on her heart patients. Dr. Blalock was too busy with his own patients, so he assigned Vivien to do the research.

Vivien headed for the Pathology Museum to investigate the collection of blue babies' hearts. He knew that a healthy heart pumps blue blood to the lungs to get oxygen. Once the blood is full of oxygen, it turns red. The red blood flows back to the heart and is delivered to every part of the body. With blue babies, however, something else was happening.

Vivien noted the four defects in the heart that blocked some of the blue blood from reaching the lungs. This meant the blood continued to circulate throughout the body without its oxygen fill-up. How do you get more blue blood to the lungs? It was a mystery Vivien was determined to solve.

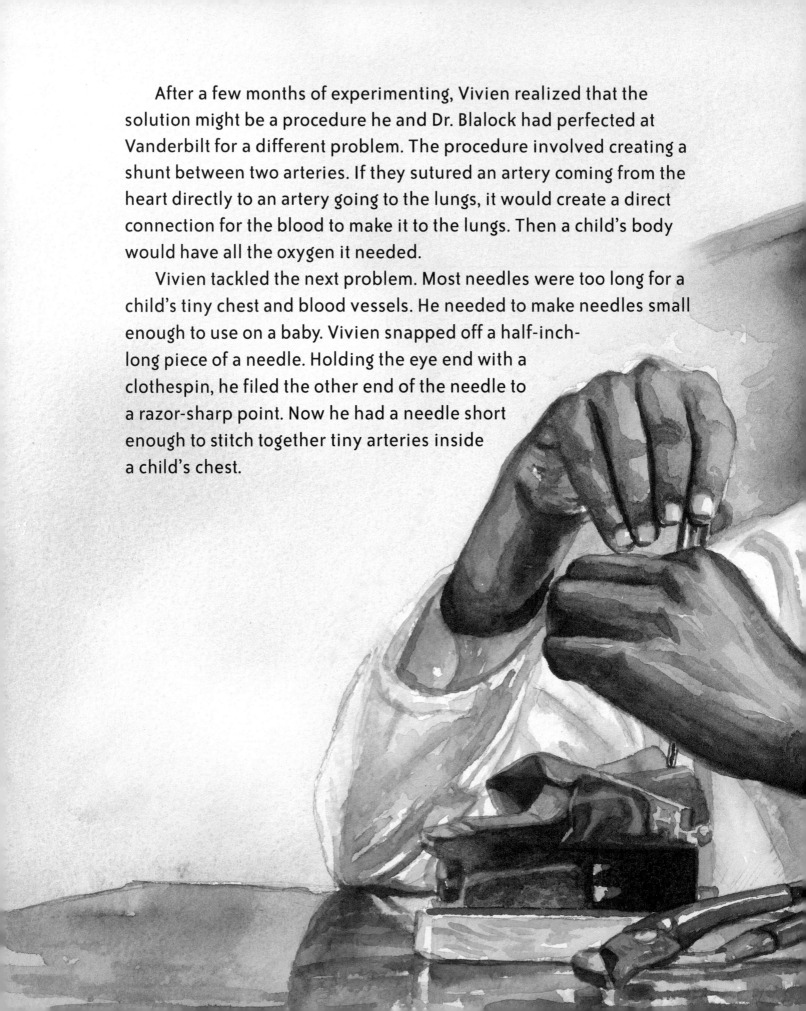

After a few months of experimenting, Vivien realized that the solution might be a procedure he and Dr. Blalock had perfected at Vanderbilt for a different problem. The procedure involved creating a shunt between two arteries. If they sutured an artery coming from the heart directly to an artery going to the lungs, it would create a direct connection for the blood to make it to the lungs. Then a child's body would have all the oxygen it needed.

Vivien tackled the next problem. Most needles were too long for a child's tiny chest and blood vessels. He needed to make needles small enough to use on a baby. Vivien snapped off a half-inch-long piece of a needle. Holding the eye end with a clothespin, he filed the other end of the needle to a razor-sharp point. Now he had a needle short enough to stitch together tiny arteries inside a child's chest.

Vivien tried out his procedure and new needles on research animals. He found a way to attach two arteries successfully and have extra blood circulate into the lungs before it flowed back to the heart and then throughout the body. Dr. Blalock assisted Vivien only once during his experiments.

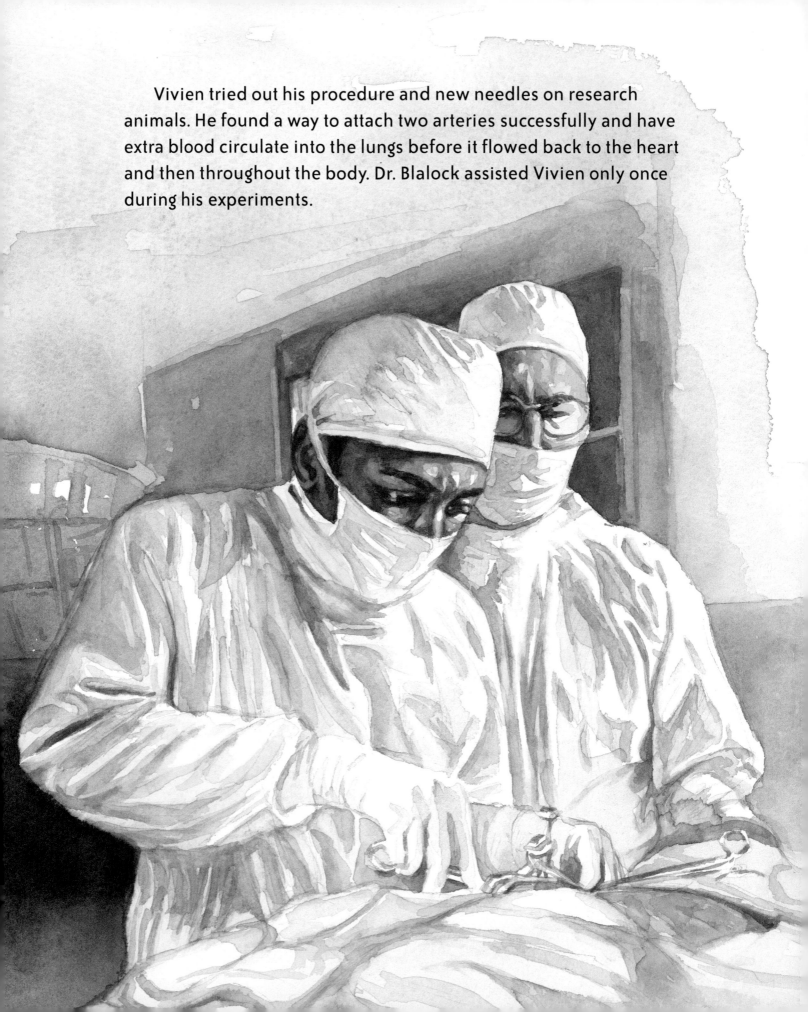

On November 29, 1944, Dr. Taussig called Dr. Blalock about Eileen, one of her blue baby patients. The child was so sick that she would die if they did not operate on her immediately.

Vivien knew his operation worked on animals, but would it work on a little girl? The next day he would find out. Dr. Blalock was going to perform the procedure designed by Vivien.

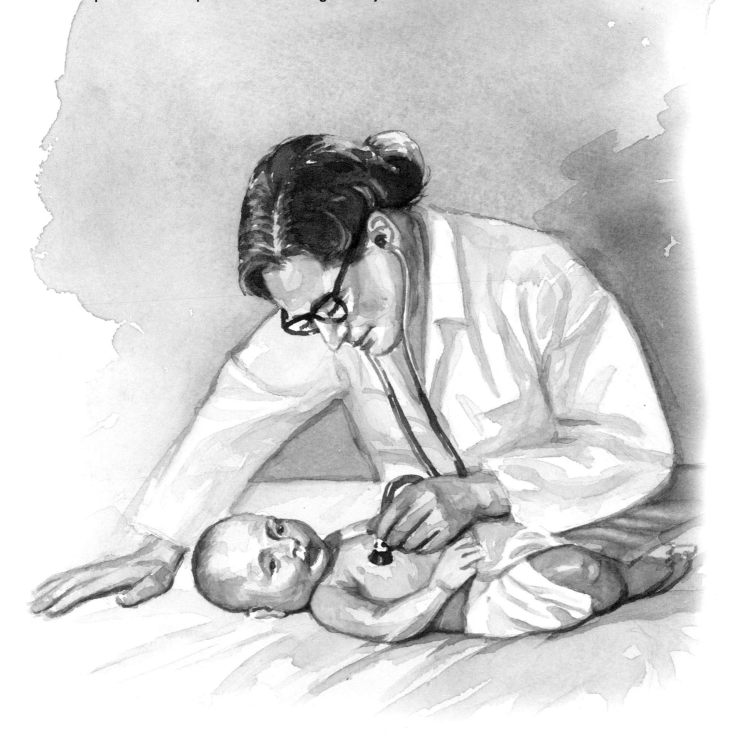

The morning of the operation, Vivien went to the operating room to check the instruments. Vivien headed back to the lab, but Dr. Blalock insisted he return to the operating room. Dr. Blalock asked Vivien to stand on a stool behind him and guide him through the operation.

Some of the other doctors grumbled, "What could Vivien possibly know?" But Vivien focused on Dr. Blalock's hands and the baby on the table.

Dr. Blalock opened Eileen's chest. Vivien's own heart thudded with worry. The baby's blood vessels were so small. Were his needles tiny enough?

Dr. Blalock began the operation.

"Is my incision long enough?" he asked Vivien.

"Yes," Vivien responded.

Dr. Blalock began a suture in the wrong direction.

"Other way," Vivien cautioned him.

Ninety minutes passed. Finally, the operation was over. Would Eileen survive?

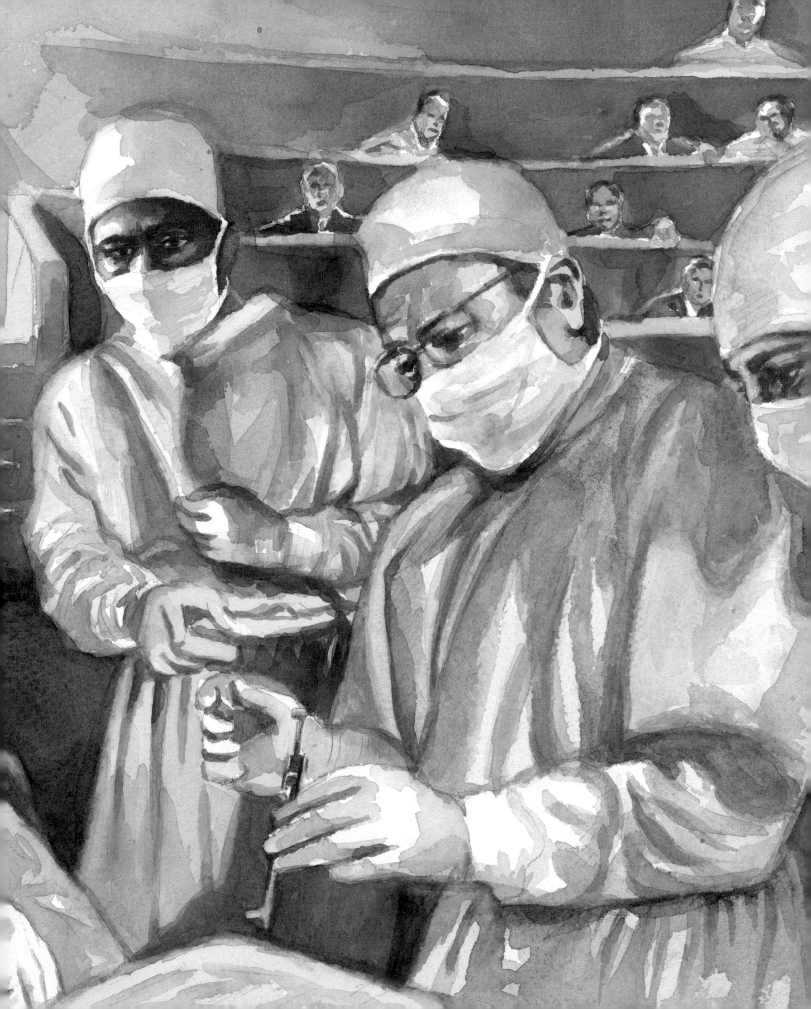

"The baby's lips are a glorious pink color!" Dr. Taussig said. Eileen did survive, and slowly, over the next few hours, her skin went from blue to a healthy pink color.

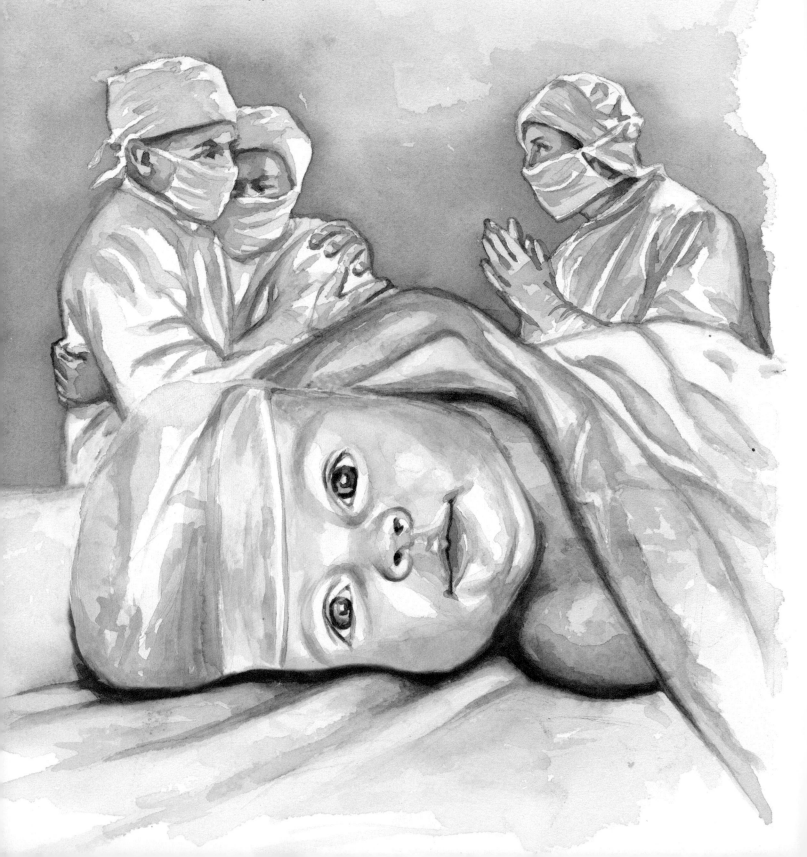

After two more successful operations, Dr. Blalock and Dr. Taussig wrote a scientific paper describing their innovative surgical procedure, which they named the Blalock-Taussig shunt. National magazines, such as *Time* and *Life*, praised Dr. Blalock and Dr. Taussig. Vivien Thomas's name did not appear anywhere in the paper or magazine articles.

As news spread of Dr. Blalock's success, two or three operations a week soon became two or three operations a day. Patients came from as far away as Europe to have the procedure. Vivien remained standing on the stool behind Dr. Blalock, coaching him through more than one hundred fifty operations.

In 1947, Dr. Blalock and Dr. Taussig were nominated for the Nobel Prize in Physiology or Medicine. Although they did not win, doctors from all over the world traveled to Johns Hopkins to observe and learn the new heart procedure. When Dr. Blalock was busy, the visiting doctors went to Vivien with their questions. Vivien graciously shared his knowledge and skills.

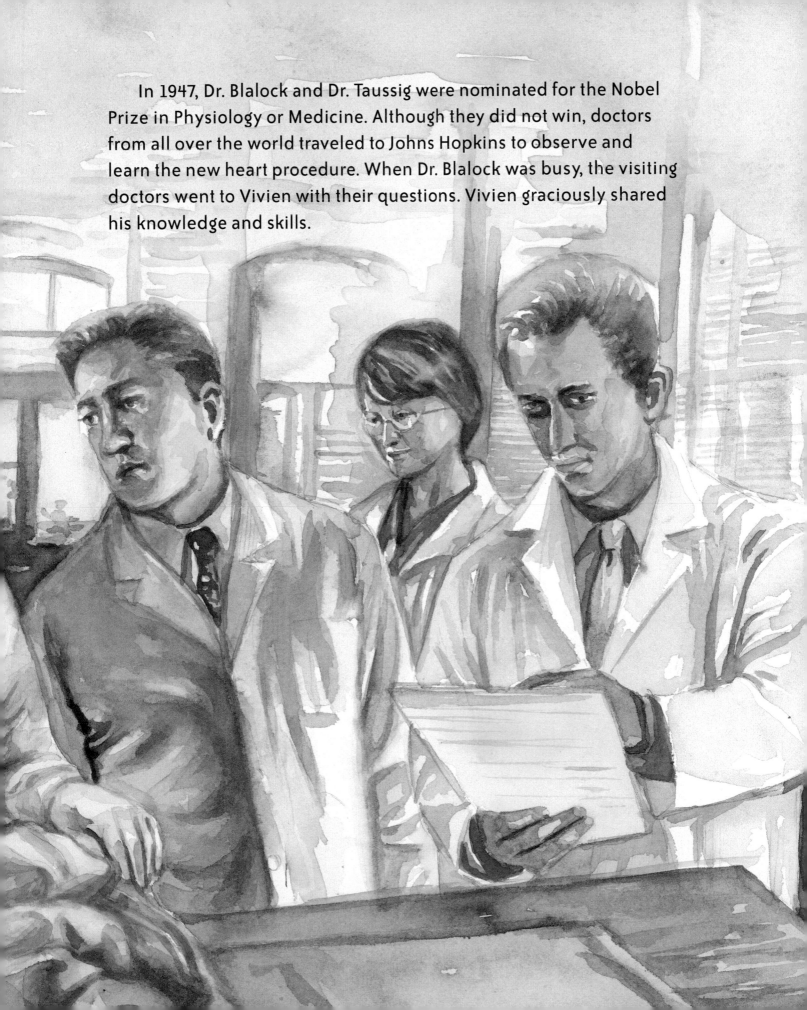

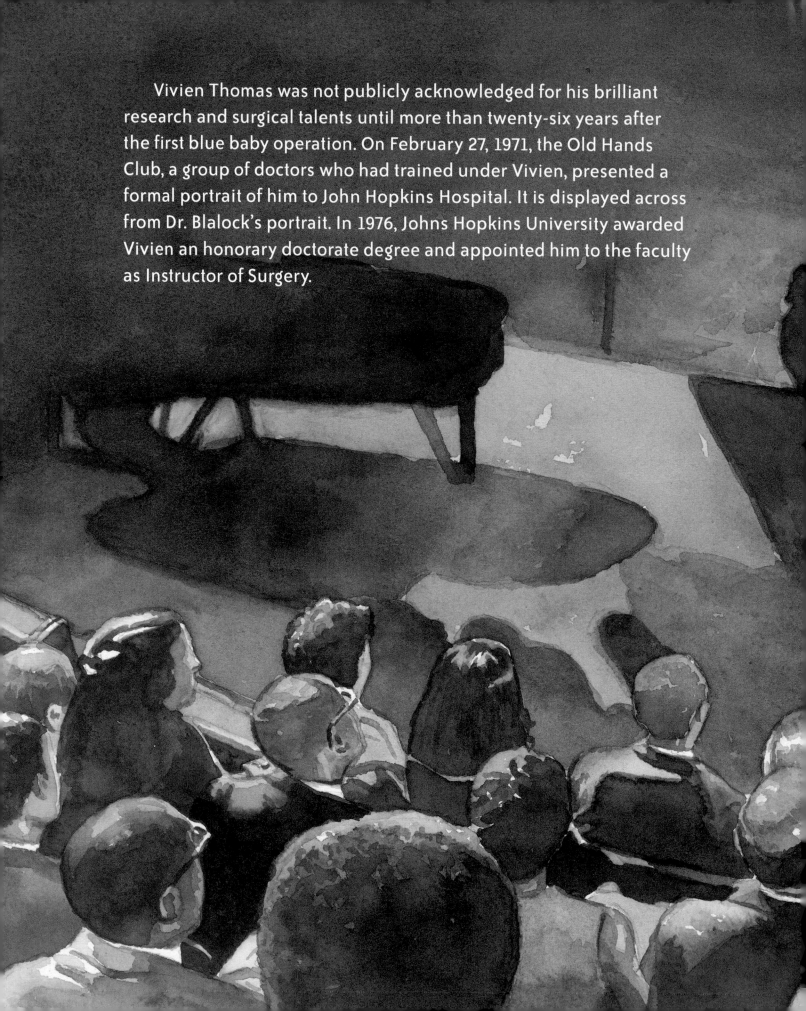

Vivien Thomas was not publicly acknowledged for his brilliant research and surgical talents until more than twenty-six years after the first blue baby operation. On February 27, 1971, the Old Hands Club, a group of doctors who had trained under Vivien, presented a formal portrait of him to John Hopkins Hospital. It is displayed across from Dr. Blalock's portrait. In 1976, Johns Hopkins University awarded Vivien an honorary doctorate degree and appointed him to the faculty as Instructor of Surgery.

Although he never had the chance to attend medical school, Vivien's research pioneered open-heart surgery on children. Today about forty thousand children are born each year with heart problems. Because of Vivien Thomas, these children now have a chance to live full and healthy lives.

MORE ABOUT TETRALOGY OF FALLOT

"Blue babies" was once a popular term, but the scientific name for the condition is "tetralogy of Fallot." Babies born with this condition have four heart defects. One defect is a hole in the wall that separates the right and left ventricles of the heart. This hole allows blood to flow back and forth between the left and right ventricles in an inefficient manner, and dilutes the supply of oxygen-rich blood to the body. Another defect involves the right ventricle. In blue babies' hearts it is much larger and thicker than in normal hearts. This overworks the heart and causes the ventricle to stiffen over time. In a third defect, the aorta, the main artery leading out of the heart, is in the wrong position. This allows the aorta to receive blood from both the right and left ventricles and mixes oxygen-poor blood with oxygen-rich blood.

Vivien Thomas decided to focus on the fourth defect: the narrowing of the flap (the pulmonary valve) that separates the right ventricle of the heart from the main blood vessel leading to the lungs. This defect limits the amount of blood that reaches the lungs. Vivien and Dr. Blalock created a shunt by joining an artery leaving the heart to an artery leading to the lungs, which allowed more blood to circulate to the lungs and then oxygenate the rest of the body.

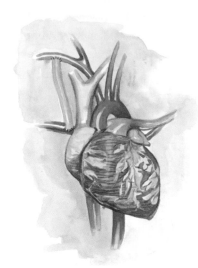

MORE ABOUT VIVIEN THOMAS

Throughout his long career, Vivien Thomas was greatly respected by other medical students for his surgical skills. He was also an inspiration to many, including Raymond Lee, who was an elevator operator at Johns Hopkins Hospital. One day while riding the elevator with Raymond, Vivien convinced him to study science. Raymond became a surgical technician and later became the first African American physician's assistant in the cardiac department at Johns Hopkins Hospital.

In 1944, Denton A. Cooley, M.D., was an intern who studied under Vivien and assisted during the first blue baby operation. In 1969, Dr. Cooley was the first doctor to implant an artificial heart in a patient. Dr. Cooley founded the Texas Heart Institute in 1962. He credits Vivien Thomas with teaching him how to turn a complicated operation into simple steps.

Dr. Rowena Spencer often assisted Vivien in the lab. Later she became the first female surgical resident and the first pediatric surgeon in Louisiana. When colleagues complimented her surgical skills, she told them about Vivien Thomas.

Despite the challenges and racial barriers he faced, Vivien made world-changing medical advances. Today a high school in Baltimore is named in his honor: the Vivien T. Thomas Medical Arts Academy. Students focus on health careers, mathematics, and the sciences.

Johns Hopkins University School of Medicine established the Vivien Thomas Fund to increase diversity and help students continue their education. The fund honors Vivien's lasting legacy and opens the door for students who otherwise may not have the chance to attend medical school.

GLOSSARY OF MEDICAL TERMS

aorta (ay-OR-tuh): main, large tube that carries blood away from the heart to the rest of the body, except the lungs

artery (AR-tuh-ree): tube that carries blood from the heart to all the other parts of the body

atrium (EH-tree-uhm): one of the two collecting chambers that transfer blood to the ventricles

blood vessel (bluhd VESS-uhl): narrow tube through which the blood flows

oxygenate (OK-si-juh-neyt): to combine with oxygen

shunt (shuhnt): surgical reconstruction or synthetic tube placed to divert blood from its normal path

ventricle (VEN-tri-kuhl): one of the two lower chambers of the heart; it receives blood from an atrium and pumps it to the arteries

AUTHOR'S SOURCES

Burkhart, Harold, M.D. "Tetralogy of Fallot in Children." Mayo Clinic, January 22, 2009. Web: March 19, 2014. http://www.youtube.com/watch?v=uPRjw8GlmoQ.

Eaton, M.D., Koco. Phone interview with nephew of Vivien Thomas. October 2011.

Elkins, M.D., Ronald C. Phone interview with colleague of Vivien Thomas. January 2012.

"Explore Tetralogy of Fallot." National Heart, Lung, and Blood Institute, July 1, 2011. http://www.nhlbi.nih.gov/health/health-topics/topics/tof.

Kehoe, Marjorie Winslow. "The Blue Baby Operation." Alan Mason Chesney Medical Archives of the Johns Hopkins Medical Institutions. http://medicalarchives.jhmi.edu/vthomas.htm.

McCabe, Katie. "Like Something the Lord Made." *The Washingtonian*, August 1989, 108–233.

Olch, Peter D., interviewer. "Vivien T. Thomas: An Oral History." U.S. National Library of Medicine, April 20, 1967. http://oculus.nlm.nih.gov/cgi/t/text/text-idx?c=oralhist;idno=2935102r.

Partners of the Heart, directed by Andrea Kalin, narrated by Morgan Freeman. Duke Media and Spark Media for PBS American Experience, 2003. DVD.

Rasmussen, Frederick N. "Vivien Thomas." *The Baltimore Sun*, May 25, 1997.

Rienzi, Greg. "Story of Legendary Johns Hopkins Team to Be Told by HBO." *The JHU Gazette* [Baltimore], May 17, 2004.

Shelley, M.D., Harry S. "Vivien Thomas." Vanderbilt University Medical School, Eskind Biomedical Library, History of Medicine Collection, March 2014. http://www.mc.vanderbilt.edu/diglib/sc_diglib/biopages/vthomas.html.

Something the Lord Made, directed by Joseph Sargent. Home Box Office (HBO), 2004. DVD.

"Tetralogy of Fallot." Mayo Clinic Staff. Mayo Clinic, February 23, 2012. http://www.mayoclinic.org/diseases-conditions/tetralogy-of-fallot/basics/definition/con-20043262.

"Tetralogy of Fallot in Children." Cincinnati Children's Hospital Medical Center, October 12, 2012. Web: March 17, 2014. http://www.cincinnatichildrens.org/health/t/tof/.

Thomas, Vivien T. *Partners of the Heart: Vivien Thomas and His Work with Alfred Blalock: An Autobiography*. Philadelphia: University of Pennsylvania, 1998.

Toledo-Pereyra, Luis H. "Something the Lord Made." *Journal of Investigative Surgery*, no. 20.2 (2007): 67–70.

"You Be the Surgeon." Tetralogy of Fallot. PBS: March 19, 2014. http://www.pbs.org/wgbh/amex/partners/breakthroughs/b_surgeon.html.

To Edmond Hooks, M.D., who made my dreams come true.
And to Anna and Will, where this journey began —G.H.

To Ronald and Norma Humphrey. I thank you both for all the help and support you
have given in making these illustrations possible —C.B.

Special thanks to Harold M. Burkhart, M.D., Pediatric Cardiovascular Surgery and Medical Director of Pediatric Cardiovascular Surgical Services at The Children's Hospital of Oklahoma, University of Oklahoma Health Sciences Center for answering questions and reading my manuscript, and for your careful attention to the tiniest detail —G.H.

LEE & LOW BOOKS Inc., 95 Madison Avenue, New York, NY 10016
leeandlow.com
Book design by Ashley Halsey
Book production by The Kids at Our House
The text is set in Baily Sans
The illustrations are rendered in watercolor

Manufactured in China by First Choice Printing Co. Ltd., January 2018
10 9 8 7 6 5 4 3
First Edition

Library of Congress Cataloging-in-Publication Data
Names: Hooks, Gwendolyn, author. | Bootman, Colin, illustrator.
Title: Tiny stitches : the life of medical pioneer Vivien Thomas / by Gwendolyn Hooks ; illustrated by Colin Bootman.
Description: First edition. | New York : Lee & Low Books Inc., [2016] | Summary: "Biography of Vivien Thomas, an African-American surgical technician who pioneered the procedure used to treat babies with a heart defect known as 'blue baby syndrome.' Includes author's note and author's sources"—Provided by publisher. | Audience: Ages 7-12. | Includes bibliographical references.
Identifiers: LCCN 2015030629 | ISBN 9781620141564 (hardcover :alk. paper)
Subjects: LCSH: Thomas, Vivien T., 1910-1985—Juvenile literature. |
Operating room technicians—Maryland—Biography—Juvenile literature. |
African American surgeons—Biography—Juvenile literature. |
Cardiovascular system—Surgery—Juvenile literature.
Classification: LCC RD99 .H66 2016 | DDC 617.4/12092—dc23
LC record available at http://lccn.loc.gov/2015030629